"WHAT DO YOU MEAN, I STILL DON'T HAVE EQUAL RIGHTS??!"

Books in the Andrews and McMeel Treasury Series

"WHAT DO YOU MEAN, I STILL DON'T HAVE EQUAL RIGHTS??!"

by Cathy Guisewite

Andrews and McMeel, Inc.
A Universal Press Sydicate Company
Kansas City • New York • Washington

ISBN: 0-8362-1158-8
Library of Congress Catalog Card Number 80-0708

I KNEW DAN WOULD SAY YES IF YOU ASKED HIM OUT.

YEAH, EXCEPT MAYBE HE JUST SAID YES BECAUSE HE COULDN'T THINK OF AN EXCUSE FAST ENOUGH.

MAYBE HE JUST **SAID** YES, AND NOW HE'S DESPERATELY TRYING TO THINK OF A WAY OUT OF IT.

MAYBE HE JUST SAID YES TO GET BACK AT A GIRL-FRIEND, AND NOW HE FEELS SO GUILTY HE'S GOING TO MAKE UP WITH HER... MAYBE.....

CATHY, WHY ARE YOU DOING THIS TO YOURSELF ?!

CAN I HELP IT IF I KNOW ALL THE OTHER THINGS THAT YES MEANS ?

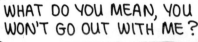

Panel 1: WHAT DO YOU MEAN, YOU WON'T GO OUT WITH ME?

Panel 2: IRVING, IT'S TAKEN ME MONTHS, BUT I'VE FINALLY REALIZED I CAN LIVE WITHOUT YOU.

IT'S TAKEN ME MONTHS TOO, CATHY.

Panel 3: BUT I'VE REALIZED I **CAN'T** LIVE WITHOUT YOU.

IRVING, LET'S FACE IT. YOU AND I ARE JUST THE KIND OF PEOPLE WHO'LL **NEVER** LIKE EACH OTHER AT THE SAME TIME.

Panel 4: WHY NOT?!

WE'RE TOO AFRAID IT MIGHT WORK.

Guisewite

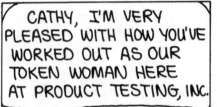

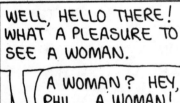

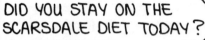

DID YOU STAY ON THE SCARSDALE DIET TODAY?

YEAH. NO PROBLEM.

YOU HAD HALF A GRAPE-FRUIT AND A SLICE OF DRY PROTEIN TOAST FOR BREAKFAST??

SORT OF. I SUBSTI-TUTED 4 DONUTS..

..AND FOR LUNCH I HAD A BIG MAC AND FRIES INSTEAD OF THE SALMON SALAD.

HA, HA, IRVING. YOU THINK YOU'RE SO SMART! WELL, YOU...

NOT BAD. I LOST 2 POUNDS.

Guisewite

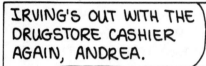

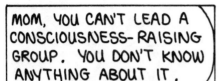

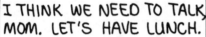

WHAT HAPPENED IN YOUR CONSCIOUSNESS-RAISING GROUP THIS MORNING?

OH, WE LEARNED ALL ABOUT ROLE-PLAYING, CATHY.

PHYLLIS DISCUSSED OUR ROLES AS WIVES AND OUR HUSBANDS' ROLES, EXCEPT FLO THOUGHT SHE WAS TALKING ABOUT **ROLLS**.

THEN OLLIE GOT EXCITED AND TOLD US ABOUT A NEW BAKERY AND WE ALL RUSHED OUT FOR DANISH.

WHAT EXACTLY DID YOU LEARN ABOUT ROLE-PLAYING, MOM?

ONLY DO IT AFTER LUNCH.

"THE WOMAN WHO REALLY SUCCEEDS IN BUSINESS TODAY IS THE WOMAN WHO KNOWS HOW TO DRESS FOR SUCCESS."

"THE PROPER CLOTHES CAN GIVE YOU AN INSTANT AURA OF CONFIDENCE, COMPETENCE AND AUTHORITY."

"INVEST IN A SERIOUS, POLISHED WARDROBE, AND YOUR RISE TO THE TOP IS VIRTUALLY ASSURED."

NOW THEY TELL ME.

ALL THIS TIME I'VE BEEN WORKING, I SHOULD HAVE BEEN SHOPPING.

Guisewite

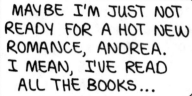

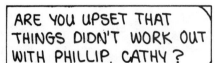

ARE YOU UPSET THAT THINGS DIDN'T WORK OUT WITH PHILLIP, CATHY?

I'M OKAY, ANDREA. OH, SURE, THERE'S DISAPPOINTMENT...

SURE THERE ARE SHATTERED HOPES.. BUT I DON'T KNOW...IN A WAY, I FEEL I REALLY ACCOMPLISHED SOMETHING.

YOU MEAN YOU LEARNED YOU'RE CAPABLE OF SAYING NO TO A RELATIONSHIP THAT DOESN'T FULFILL YOUR INTELLECTUAL NEEDS?

NO. I BROKE UP BEFORE THERE WAS ANYTHING OF HIS I HAD TO RETURN.

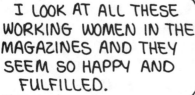

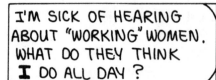

HOW WAS YOUR CONSCIOUS-NESS-RAISING SESSION ON "DEVELOPING SELF-RESPECT", MOM?

IT WENT VERY WELL UNTIL I SERVED THE REFRESHMENTS.

ALL THE WOMEN STARTED FIGHTING OVER WHO GOT TO EAT THE BROKEN COOKIES.

OH, THAT'S PERFECT.

WHAT A PERFECT TIME TO DISCUSS THE LINK BE-TWEEN SELF-RESPECT AND THE FACT THAT MOTHERS CAN'T STAND TO EAT COOKIES THAT AREN'T BROKEN!!... WHAT DID YOU SAY TO THEM??

STAND BACK, LADIES! I'M GOING TO SMASH ALL THE COOKIES SO WE CAN REALLY ENJOY OURSELVES!!

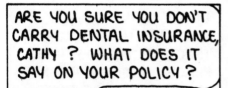

ARE YOU SURE YOU DON'T CARRY DENTAL INSURANCE, CATHY ? WHAT DOES IT SAY ON YOUR POLICY ?

HOW SHOULD I KNOW ?

CATHY... DIDN'T YOU READ YOUR INSURANCE POLICY AS SOON AS YOU GOT IT ??

NO. I STUFFED IT IN A DRAWER WITH MY OTHER INSURANCE POLICIES.

YOU **NEVER** READ YOUR HEALTH INSURANCE POLICY ?!

I NEVER READ **ANY** OF MY INSURANCE POLICIES, ANDREA.

I ALWAYS THOUGHT I WAS PRETTY AMAZING FOR KEEPING THEM IN THE SAME DRAWER.

DUE TO HEAVY AIR TRAVEL, ALL LINES ARE BUSY. YOUR CALL WILL BE ANSWERED IN THE ORDER RECEIVED BY AN OVER-WORKED, GROUCHY RESERVATIONIST.

DO NOT HANG UP. IT'S A MIRACLE THAT YOU GOT THROUGH IN THE FIRST PLACE, AND YOU'RE NOT LIKELY TO HAVE THAT KIND OF LUCK AGAIN.

IN FACT, IF YOU TRY TO CALL BACK LATER, YOU WILL GET A BUSY SIGNAL 450 TIMES IN A ROW. THIS IS THE ONLY RECORDED MESSAGE YOU WILL HEAR.

THANK GOODNESS.

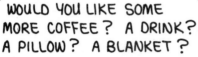

GO OUT ON THE TOWN NOW? YOU'RE CRAZY. AREN'T YOU EXHAUSTED FROM SKIING ALL DAY??

HAH! YOU WOMEN HAVE NO STAMINA.

SKI-BAR

WE BOOGIED ALL DAY AND NOW WE'RE GOING TO BOOGIE ALL NIGHT! YAHOO! LET'S GET ROWDY!! LET'S PARTY DOWN!!

ZZZZZ

ZZZZZ

THUNK!

THUNK!

WHY IS THE WOMAN WITH NO STAMINA ALWAYS THE LAST ONE STANDING UP?

ZZZZ

ZZZZ

©husewitz

ISN'T IT INTERESTING THAT WHEN YOU MEET SOMEONE, ALL THE CONVERSATION SEEMS SHALLOW UNTIL YOU TALK ABOUT THAT PERSON'S RELATIONSHIPS WITH OTHER PEOPLE?

I MEAN, YOU CAN SAY ANYTHING, BUT IT'S ONLY WHEN YOU DISCUSS PAST INVOLVEMENTS OR FUTURE INVOLVEMENTS THAT THE CONVERSATION BECOMES REALLY "MEANINGFUL."

IT'S AMAZING, ISN'T IT? JUST KNOWING ABOUT THE PERSON AS A PERSON-- AN INDIVIDUAL--IS NEVER ENOUGH.

I HATE IT WHEN I WASTE A GREAT REVELATION ON A SIX-YEAR-OLD.

I KNOW I SAID I WANTED TO GET AWAY FROM YOU... BUT I'VE BEEN GONE 10 DAYS. I THOUGHT I'D HEAR **SOMETHING.**

I MEAN, YOU DIDN'T CALL, YOU DIDN'T WRITE.. OF COURSE I FEEL REJECTED.

I THOUGHT I WAS MORE IMPORTANT TO YOU THAN THAT ! I THOUGHT YOU NEEDED ME !!

WHO WAS THAT ? YOUR BOYFRIEND ?

NO. MY OFFICE.

OH, LOOK, CATHY. THE "ME" DECADE IS ALL OVER NOW.

"THE WILD SELF-INDULGENCE AND CRAZY, CAREFREE HEDONISM OF THE 70's ARE GIVING WAY TO A MORE SENSIBLE, DOWN-TO-EARTH KIND OF LIFESTYLE."

I'M STARTING TO GET THE FEELING I MISSED SOMETHING BIG.

IRVING, I'M CALLING TO PLEAD WITH YOU TO NOT READ THE LETTER YOU GOT FROM ME TODAY.

THE LETTER WAS WRITTEN AT THE HEIGHT OF A MANIAC EMOTIONAL CRISIS. IT'S FULL OF HORRIBLE, EMBARRASSING SENTIMENTS.

I ATTACKED YOU AND YOUR NEW GIRLFRIEND IN THE MOST PERSONAL WAY... IRVING, I USED WORDS I HAD TO LOOK UP IN THE DICTIONARY!

WHAT DID HE SAY, CATHY?

I COULDN'T HEAR OVER THE SOUND OF HIM RIPPING THE ENVELOPE OPEN.

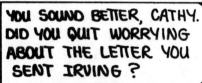

YOU SOUND BETTER, CATHY. DID YOU QUIT WORRYING ABOUT THE LETTER YOU SENT IRVING?

NO, ANDREA. BUT I DID DECIDE TO PUT THAT NEGATIVE ENERGY TO WORK.

THEY SAY THAT WHEN YOU'RE REALLY UPSET, THE BEST THERAPY IS TO START DOING SOMETHING CONSTRUCTIVE, LIKE CLEANING THE HOUSE.

YOU NOT ONLY WORK OFF THE ANXIETIES, BUT YOU CAN ACCOMPLISH GREAT THINGS!

THAT'S FABULOUS, CATHY. WHAT HAVE YOU ACCOMPLISHED SO FAR?

I THREW THE VACUUM CLEANER THROUGH THE WALL.

Guisewite

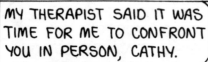

"YOUR 1980 GUIDE TO TAX LAWS AND LOOPHOLES..."

"...380 BIG PAGES CRAMMED WITH LEGAL WAYS TO SAVE THOUSANDS OF DOLLARS ON YOUR INCOME TAX RETURNS."

"...IF YOU ARE STILL SINGLE AND EARN LESS THAN $35,000 A YEAR, NOT ONE WORD OF THIS BOOK WILL APPLY."

I DON'T KNOW WHETHER TO BE MAD THAT I DON'T QUALIFY OR HAPPY THAT I DON'T HAVE TO READ THE BOOK.

Guisewite

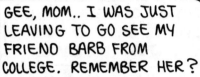

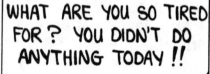